Rejoice always, pray continually,
give thanks in all circumstances;
for this is God's will for you in Christ Jesus.

1 THESSALONIANS 5:16-18 NIV

Gratitude is the companion to worship. We turn our eyes to the Giver with worship, and we acknowledge His gifts to us, His favor on us, with gratitude. We may not see what we hope to see God doing, but we don't want to miss all that He is doing.

FROM *MAKING PEACE WITH CHANGE* BY GINA BRENNA BUTZ

You open your hand and satisfy the desires of every living thing.

PSALM 145:16 NIV

Every good and perfect gift is from above,
coming down from the Father of the heavenly lights,
who does not change like shifting shadows.

JAMES 1:17 NIV

From start to finish, the Bible not only makes much of God, it encourages its readers to do likewise. We're to give thanks (Psalm 107) in all things (1 Thessalonians 5:18). We're to find joy in focusing on who God is and all He has done to rescue and redeem us. Ask God to help you cultivate a heart that sees the majesty of God all around you.

FROM *101 IMPORTANT WORDS OF THE BIBLE* BY LEN WOODS

_____

_____

_____

_____

_____

_____

_____

_____

_____

_____

_____

_____

_____

_____

_____

_____

_____

_____

_____

Give thanks to the LORD, for he is good! His faithful love endures
forever. Has the LORD redeemed you? Then speak out!

PSALM 107:1–2 NLT

_____

_____

_____

_____

_____

_____

_____

_____

_____

_____

_____

_____

_____

_____

_____

_____

_____

_____

_____

_____

_____

_____

Oh, how my soul praises the Lord. How my spirit rejoices
in God my Savior! . . . For the Mighty One is holy,
and he has done great things for me.

LUKE 1:46-47, 49 NLT

Make a joyful noise to the LORD, all the earth! Serve the LORD
with gladness! Come into his presence with singing! Know
that the LORD, he is God! It is he who made us, and we are
his; we are his people, and the sheep of his pasture.

PSALM 100:1-3 ESV

_____

_____

_____

_____

_____

_____

_____

_____

_____

_____

Devote yourselves to prayer, being watchful and thankful.
(Colossians 4:2 NIV)

Be watchful and thankful. When we pray, we don't fling requests up to heaven and forget them. Instead, God calls us to pray and watch for answers. And while we sow the seeds of prayer and wait for God to produce a harvest, we soften and till the ground with our expressions of thanksgiving.

It's an awesome privilege to bring our requests before the King of Kings and Lord of Lords and know we'll always have an audience. We can thank Him for responding to our prayers with wisdom and love, believing that His heart seeks only two things: our good and His glory. And finally (this takes mature faith), we thank Him for answering no to some of our prayers, trusting that He knows best.

FROM *REFRESH YOUR FAITH* BY LORI HATCHER

Oh, taste and see
that the LORD is good.

PSALM 34:8 NKJV

_____

_____

_____

_____

_____

_____

_____

Today when you pray, set aside your lists and focus on God. Praise Him for His attributes. Thank Him for His work in your life. Reflect on His majesty. Enjoy His presence. Remember His history of faithfulness through the ages. Listen to Him speak to you through the voice of the Holy Spirit and His Word. Enter into the fellowship already taking place between the Father, Son, and Holy Spirit. (from *Refresh Your Prayers* by Lori Hatcher)

ASPECTS OF GOD'S CHARACTER I'M THANKFUL FOR:

-
-
-
-
-

You have turned my mourning into joyful dancing. . . .
God, I will give you thanks forever!

PSALM 30:11-12 NLT

_____

_____

_____

_____

_____

_____

_____

_____

_____

_____

_____

_____

_____

_____

_____

_____

_____

_____

_____

_____

_____

_____

_____

Is anyone among you suffering? Let him pray.
Is anyone cheerful? Let him sing psalms.

JAMES 5:13 NKJV

_____

_____

_____

_____

_____

_____

_____

_____

_____

Do not be anxious about anything, but in every situation, by prayer and petition, with thanksgiving, present your requests to God. And the peace of God, which transcends all understanding, will guard your hearts and your minds in Christ Jesus. (Philippians 4:6–7 NIV)

He says specifically to not be anxious about anything—our future, our concern, our habit. Nothing. When anxiety comes, we can do as Paul suggests: pray. And he says to pray with thanksgiving, remembering all we have to be thankful for. Paul's prescription forces our minds off of our concerns and shifts them to all we have to be thankful for. It's a mind change—an intentional decision to focus on what we have to be thankful for. . . . No, your situation may not change instantly, but you can change and allow peace and gratitude to calm your nerves and shift your focus.

FROM _NAVIGATING THE BLUES_ BY KATARA WASHINGTON PATTON

My heart is confident in you, O God; my heart is confident.
No wonder I can sing your praises! Wake up, my heart! Wake up, O
lyre and harp! I will wake the dawn with my song. I will thank you, Lord.

PSALM 57:7-9 NLT

It is good to give thanks to the LORD, to sing praises to
your name, O Most High; to declare your steadfast love
in the morning, and your faithfulness by night.

PSALM 92:1-2 ESV

The LORD is my strength and my song.

EXODUS 15:2 NLT

I called for help,
and you listened to my cry.

JONAH 2:2 NIV

According to His trustworthy character, God transforms our prayers from desperate pleas for provision to grateful praises for His *promised* provision. We can expect Him to take care of us because His Word says that He will. He is *Jehovah-Jireh*, a name that means "God Will Provide." Waiting won't always be easy or worry-free, but the process can lead to joyful expectation of God's dependability and the glorious exaltation of His name.

FROM *WAITING FOR GOD* BY XOCHITL DIXON

_____

_____

_____

_____

_____

_____

_____

_____

_____

_____

_____

_____

_____

_____

_____

_____

_____

_____

_____

_____

_____

_____

_____

_____

I praise your name for your unfailing love and faithfulness;
for your promises are backed by all the honor of your name.

PSALM 138:2 NLT

As you therefore have received Christ Jesus the Lord, so walk
in Him, rooted and built up in Him and established in the faith,
as you have been taught, abounding in it with thanksgiving.

COLOSSIANS 2:6-7 NKJV

The discipline of thanksgiving, honoring the simple blessings of daily life . . . is a good spiritual practice because we sometimes forget how the Lord has sustained us even through difficult moments. God brought you through the divorce, that deployment, the miscarriage, the loss of a dear friend, the rejection, the abuse, the lies, the grief, the depression. We sometimes forget that God is at work in our abilities. God made it possible for the degree, the certification, the job promotion, the opportunity that fell in your lap. God is the one who sustains the earth and protects us from dangers we cannot see. God is the reason that despite our abuse, the earth has not burned up yet. He is the reason that you didn't fall asleep at the wheel, weren't born at a different period in history, and did not crash in your plane. As a personal reflection, take time this week to record and give thanks for God's faithfulness to you over the years. (from *Journey to Freedom* by Natasha Sistrunk Robinson)

WAYS GOD HAS BEEN
FAITHFUL TO ME:

-
-
-
-
-
-
-

You are entirely faithful.

PSALM 89:8 NLT

The steadfast love of the LORD never ceases;
his mercies never come to an end; they are new every morning.

LAMENTATIONS 3:22-23 ESV

Because your love is better than life,
my lips will glorify you. I will
praise you as long as I live.

PSALM 63:3-4 NIV

I lift up my eyes to the mountains—
    where does my help come from?
My help comes from the LORD,
    the Maker of heaven and earth.

He will not let your foot slip—
    he who watches over you will not slumber;
indeed, he who watches over Israel
    will neither slumber nor sleep.

The LORD watches over you—
    the LORD is your shade at your right hand;
the sun will not harm you by day,
    nor the moon by night.

The LORD will keep you from all harm—
    he will watch over your life;
the LORD will watch over your coming and going
    both now and forevermore. (Psalm 121 NIV)

Psalm 121. The pilgrims look up at the hills of Jerusalem with anticipation, and they are reminded of the source of their help: "the LORD, the Maker of heaven and earth" (v. 2). How can we resist worshiping One who can fling the universe into existence with His voice yet still cares enough that He watches over us? "The LORD watches over you. . . . The LORD will watch over your coming and going both now and forevermore" (vv. 5, 8). What else can we do but respond in awe?

FROM *LIVING THE PSALMS LIFE* BY DAVE BRANON

Since we are receiving a Kingdom that is unshakable, let us be thankful and please God by worshiping him with holy fear and awe.

HEBREWS 12:28 NLT

Whatever you do, in word or deed, do everything in the name of the Lord Jesus, giving thanks to God the Father through him.

COLOSSIANS 3:17 ESV

As the heavens are higher
than the earth, so are My ways
higher than your ways.

ISAIAH 55:9 NKJV

_____

_____

_____

_____

_____

_____

_____

Can you recall a time when God answered a prayer completely differently than you'd hoped or considered, but He definitely answered? Write about it here. End your journaling with these words: "Give thanks to the Lord. His love endures forever." (from *Restore My Soul* by Laura L. Smith)

GOD ANSWERED MY PRAYER BY . . .

-
-
-
-
-
-

_____

_____

_____

_____

_____

_____

_____

_____

_____

_____

_____

_____

_____

_____

He remembered us in our weakness.
His faithful love endures forever.
He saved us from our enemies.
His faithful love endures forever.
He gives food to every living thing.
His faithful love endures forever.
Give thanks to the God of heaven.
His faithful love endures forever.

PSALM 136:23–26 NLT

God of Surprises, your story of redemption shows you are a God who does the unexpected in unexpected ways. You use the unlikely to tell your story, and you are continuing to tell it, with and through us. Thank you for allowing us to be a part of it. I confess that sometimes I think I know what the next scene should be. My expectations threaten to change the script from your story to mine. Forgive me for the times when I thought I knew precisely what you were doing. Forgive me for not following the leading of your Spirit. Help me to recognize when my expectations are coloring my understanding. Help me to play my part in your redemption story. Amen.

FROM *ENCOUNTERS WITH JESUS* BY J.R. HUDBERG

But I trust in your unfailing love;

my heart rejoices in your salvation.

PSALM 13:5 NIV

My God will meet all your needs according to
the riches of his glory in Christ Jesus.

PHILIPPIANS 4:19 NIV

What we have in God is far more significant than what we get from God. This is perhaps why so many of us struggle with the idea of contentment. Especially in western cultures, contentment is secured by accumulation of things—but there is never enough. Accumulation of things is like drinking salt water; it only leaves us thirsty for more. And more. And more.

Contentment for the child of God is not based on what we have but rather on whose we are and who He is. It is this fundamental reality that fuels how our hearts are to process life in an often unfair world. It is not simply about what He does or what He provides, it is about who He is. Hebrews 13:5 says to be "content with what you have; for He Himself has said, 'I will never desert you, nor will I ever forsake you'" (NASB).

FROM *GOD OF SURPRISE* BY BILL CROWDER

God remains the strength of my heart; he is mine forever.

PSALM 73:26 NLT

Thanking our Savior is the natural response to having been forgiven by our Savior.

FROM *THE PARABLES* BY GARY INRIG

You make known to me the path of life; in your presence there is fullness of joy; at your right hand are pleasures forevermore.

PSALM 16:11 ESV

_____

_____

_____

_____

_____

_____

_____

_____

_____

_____

_____

_____

_____

_____

_____

_____

Real gratitude causes us to make an effort to come back to God. There's a choice to be made. We can go our own way distracted by all God has given us, or we can fall at Jesus's feet and worship Him for what He has done. Do that, and you'll find He gives you even more.

Keep your eyes on the gift and (maybe) you'll be blessed as long as it lasts. Turn your heart to the Giver, and you'll be blessed for eternity.

FROM *PRAYING THE PRAYERS OF THE BIBLE* BY JAMES BANKS

Giving thanks is a sacrifice that truly honors me. If you keep to my path, I will reveal to you the salvation of God.

PSALM 50:23 NLT

Bless the LORD, O my soul, and all that is within me, bless his holy name!... Forget not all his benefits, who forgives all your iniquity, who heals all your diseases, who redeems your life from the pit, who crowns you with steadfast love and mercy.

PSALM 103:1-4 ESV

SOURCES

Banks, James. *Praying the Prayers of the Bible*. Grand Rapids, MI: Our Daily Bread Publishing, 2013.

Branon, Dave. *Living the Psalms Life: 10 Guiding Principles for Fellowship with God*. Grand Rapids, MI: Our Daily Bread Publishing, 2019.

Butz, Gina Brenna. *Making Peace with Change: Navigating Life's Messy Transitions with Honesty and Grace*. Grand Rapids, MI: Our Daily Bread Publishing, 2020.

Crowder, Bill. *God of Surprise: The Life-Changing, Unexpected Ways God Works for Our Good*. Grand Rapids, MI: Our Daily Bread Publishing, 2020.

Dixon, Xochitl. *Waiting for God: Trusting Daily in God's Plan and Pace*. Grand Rapids, MI: Our Daily Bread Publishing, 2019.

Hatcher, Lori. *Refresh Your Faith: Uncommon Devotions from Every Book of the Bible*. Grand Rapids, MI: Our Daily Bread Publishing, 2020.

———. *Refresh Your Prayers: Uncommon Devotions to Restore Power and Praise*. Grand Rapids, MI: Our Daily Bread Publishing, 2022.

Hudberg, J.R. *Encounters with Jesus: Forty Reflections on Knowing and Loving the Savior*. Grand Rapids, MI: Our Daily Bread Publishing, 2022.

Inrig, Gary. *The Parables: Understanding What Jesus Meant*. Grand Rapids, MI: Our Daily Bread Publishing, 1991.

Patton, Katara Washington. *Navigating the Blues: Where to Turn When Worry, Anxiety, or Depression Steal Your Hope*. Grand Rapids, MI: Our Daily Bread Publishing, 2022.

Robinson, Natasha Sistrunk. *Journey to Freedom: Discovering the God of Deliverance, An Exodus Bible Study*. Grand Rapids, MI: Our Daily Bread Publishing, 2022.

Smith, Laura L. *Restore My Soul: The Power and Promise of 30 Psalms*. Grand Rapids, MI: Our Daily Bread Publishing, 2022.

Woods, Len. *101 Important Words of the Bible: And the Unforgettable Story They Tell*. Grand Rapids, MI: Our Daily Bread Publishing, 2020.

PERMISSIONS AND CREDITS

For more resources from Our Daily Bread Publishing, visit odb.org/store.